BROTHER POEM

T0025765

BROTHER POEM
Will Harris

WESLEYAN UNIVERSITY PRESS
Middletown, Connecticut

Wesleyan University Press
Middletown CT 06459
www.wesleyan.edu/wespress

First published in Great Britain by Granta Poetry in 2023

Manufactured in the United States of America
Typeset in Minion by Hamish Ironside
Front cover illustration and design by David Pearson

The acknowledgements on pages 86 and 87 constitute
an extension of this copyright page.

Image on page 66 courtesy of the Prokudin-Gorskiĭ photograph
collection, Library of Congress, Prints and Photographs Division

Library of Congress Cataloging-In-Publication Data
NAMES: Harris, Will, author.
TITLE: Brother poem / Will Harris.
OTHER TITLES: Brother poem (Compilation)
DESCRIPTION: Middletown, Connecticut : Wesleyan University
    Press, [2023] | Series: Wesleyan poetry | Summary: "Poems
    whose central concern is a series of addresses to an absent
    brother, where the impossibility of speech comes to prefigure a
    different sort of kinship, one that extends beyond speech, which
    is intimate and communal, grieving and joyful, and endless"—
    Provided by publisher.
IDENTIFIERS: LCCN 2022047664 (print) | LCCN 2022047665 (ebook)
    | ISBN 9780819500526 (trade paperback) | ISBN 9780819500564
    (ebook)
SUBJECTS: BISAC: POETRY / Subjects & Themes / Family | POETRY /
    Subjects & Themes / Places
CLASSIFICATION: LCC PR6108.A769 B76 2023 (print) | LCC PR6108.
    A769 (ebook) | DDC 821/.92 — dc23/eng/20221207
LC record available at https://lccn.loc.gov/2022047664
LC ebook record available at https://lccn.loc.gov/2022047665

5 4 3 2 1

There stands the stump; with foreign voices other
willows converse, beneath our, beneath those skies,
and I am hushed, as if I'd lost a brother.
– ANNA AKHMATOVA, 'Willow' (trans. JENNIFER REESER)

CONTENTS

In June, outrageous stood the flagons on
the pavement which extended to the river
where we spoke of everything except
the fear that would, when habit ended, be
depended on. Our fear of darkness as
the fear of darkness never ending. To
hell with it, you said, and why not? Let's buy
a dirty and slobbery farm in Albion. What
country is this? There was the big loom
we little mice were born to tarry in.
Its patter made the bad things better. O
we sang against the light as we sang
against the battens! Cold that June and mist-
shapen, the river mind and all else matter,
I called you. Where are you? It's getting
dark. But these being statements, they ran
away before I could say *hummock coastline theft*.
This is where we used to speak of everything.
I need one more hour please. One more
hour. My affordable memories sold, I hung
my phone from the highest flagpole and kissed
the face of England once discreetly, though
it wasn't you and neither was the mist
wherefrom in dingle darkness buzzed a single
notification. Call me when you get this.
And see I'm calling now, whether or not
this is *now* or *in time*.

Cuttlefish

We were sitting on the floor. I started writing
as the window darkened and the grass grew
bright. By morning, half the trees were
submarine. What was it about being young and
wanting to write? You said it wasn't choice, it
was dictation: you had to ask. A frog leapt

through the cat flap taking refuge by our feet.
You knew I had a brother though we'd only met
that night. Each time you forget and remember
the experience becomes truer. Like lightning
in reverse the fuse blew. I was stirring a pot
of dal, your dog Annie asleep on the floor beside

me, snoring. We went to a cafe whose name
rhymed with dal, me playing with a small
salt shaker, you talking about your brother. He had
to go and you were about to go with him but
then you changed your mind. There was an
accident that night. One second he was in his car

asking if you wanted to go and you were about to
and that was that. We were strangers in a circle eating
peach cobbler. Someone played 'Galway Girl' on
a child's toy guitar. It's me! It's me! you screamed
because you used to live on Grafton St in Boston. Too
late to leave and raining now, we talked about

your brother. It was after college that you started
writing. Lightning crackled in the air. You were all
along me. I watched you heat a pot of dal, your dog
asleep beside you. You'd planned to leave by
twenty-three but changed your mind. To talk with
shadows you became a shade. Your eyes were

red, you looked like him. I didn't know you had
a brother. You had to ask, you don't have to believe.
We were sitting on our parents' couch. I said it
wasn't choice. You were my brother. We were
events in language. The window darkened and
the grass grew bright. Can you hear that, Cuttlefish?

In Anxiety Dreams

Not seeing you had made it easier to talk.
And I liked that while we talked I could
look outside, only once checking my phone
for messages. The shadow of my foot
waved at me from the wall. With foreign
voices other willows conversed. Too many
tree analogies, you said. But by then I
had a whole book of them, of which this
was the first. I do it when I'm anxious. I'm
always falling backwards, my suitcase falling
with me. The cops waiting.

                This time we
were on a boat, which was maybe awkward
to say because it was meant to be a poem
about trees and falling, the kind of dream that
wakes you when you're anxious. Said to be
due to an arm falling away from the body
or a flexed knee suddenly extended
at a time when the sense of cutaneous
pressure is becoming less conscious. But
in dreams what's *said to be* is less important
than what's said and nothing important
can be said. We were ordering pizza. You
were looking at gifs. What use are sycamores?

    It was always April in this mood. No
condition on it such as resting implies.

You told me once I think it was in Denmark
it rained fish because the sun dehydrated
the water and took it up into the atmosphere
and rehydrated the fish eggs and they hatched
so it rained fish. I never asked you what
it meant, only what wish it expressed.

Does it matter in the fluid-filled way
of things that float up to the surface whether
or not we talk, half of you facing away from
half of me as in a painting by Carlotti, a
posture of admission and defeat? I want
to speak, but also to wander at peace myself
outdoors a green tree reading in the free air
having had the elements in me, language
porous with battered lapsed impossible
things. And after some time like this, though
I don't have much, I want to come back.

The shadow of my foot waved at me
from the door. At the junction we were
running late when I fell backwards, a sheaf
of images spilling under me: of decision
points, of rotten gums, of defunct operating
systems, of English trees. But having nothing
to say I felt relief. The freedom of an oak tree
with its roots in invisible space. I knew
this pain would pass. With foreign voices
other willows conversed. Precordial leaves.
And I was quiet, as if I'd lost a brother.

After 'The Quinine Plant'

The more he thought

> the more thinking
> itself became
> a source of anxiety
> casting its green
> shade over him
> mid-sleep because
> of what he was
> and could not be
> because of what
> he did not know
> he was

> London he knew
> it was the other
> country in him
> he feared
> the oak tree's unseen
> roots whose
> tendrils poked out
> mid-speech

> did you inhale
> diaspora did you
> choose cliché
> no
> he said
> not knowingly

The more he thought

                                        the more things
                                        came back to him
                                        like the myth
                                        of the great-
                                        great-grandmother
                                        who left Fujian
                                        on broken feet
                                        sometime in the late
                                        Qing dynasty
                                        the myth of the living
                                        tree divided
                                        among her children
                                        who became many
                                        distinct seeds that
                                        when cashed
                                        became
                                        one currency

The more he thought

the more he had to move
and soon he found himself
in Beijing expecting
the thud of recognition
but as in a dream
he moved differently
walking the hutongs
at night shop after shop
different but the same
he licked toffee apples
and drank bubble tea
his feet never touching
real earth

The more he thought

the more names appeared
Pekanbaru
Kota Bharu
Chiang Mai
places whose names
meant something new
and that was when
he remembered
'The Quinine Plant'
the poem he'd spent
years writing then
abandoned
and he thought of
the plant's long waxy
leaves and white purplish
flowers cultivated
by the Dutch as
a vaccine for malaria
in the late nineteenth century
when his own Dutch
great-great-grandfather
worked at a quinine plant
in Bandung

The more he thought

                                        the more he needed to return
                                           to Peking University's
                                        gated campus where aged five
                                           he and his mum had lived
                                              for ten months

                                              a guard stopped him
                                            at the gates to ask for ID
                                           just as a different man who
                                               looked like a svelte
                                                  Santa Claus
                                               appeared and said
                                                he was a professor
                                                  of economics
                                               he'd vouch for him

The more he thought

the less he knew
sitting beside
the artificial lake
a part of him
remembered it
twenty-five years before
snowed under dirty-
white as swan's down
the other part
connecting nothing
with nothing as
the sun set
behind a plate of
green smog

The more he thought

the more he returned to
'The Quinine Plant' as a way to make
sense of his parents' relationship
as a kind of postcolonial romance
which made him its awkward
postscript

The more he thought

the less he could extract
some life-saving
balm from the duress
of history
without which
what was the point
of poetry

The more he thought

the less order took the form
of words to represent
the slaughter his family
escaped the more
he thought of buckets
of fried chicken
his uncle brought back
from KFC when
he worked there
in Anaheim
in the late '90s
his cousin already
speaking perfect
American

he saw his uncle's
sweat-stained
armpits
as he praised
Colonel Sanders

have more
biscuit
have more
gravy

The more he thought

the more he needed to purge
himself through walking
at night inhaling tree pollen
thrown into the air
by recent rain
so he walked until
his eyes were bleared until
he had to lie down
on wet grass dreaming
the pages of
'The Quinine Plant'
buried in a green
shade and grown tall
with the blood of workers
a violent plant
which occasionally
bore small flowers
that smelt of
milk sweets and made
white people
salivate
though unfortunately
they were
poisonous

Free Will

Letting the bath run I sat on the toilet and thought about
keeping the plug in till the water spilt which made me think if all
things have as their cause what happened how can you change
course, prior will spilling through you or some unseen drain blocked
with gunk, like in the case of cloves it wasn't that the smell drove the
Dutch to kill and pillage but that it told them they were nearly there
and maybe would do anything to get it, it being what would spill
through them unabated. The last time we met I tried to smell what the
Dutch smelt, the air full of burning cloves, the crematorium guard
smoking clove cigarettes, smoke rising from him like the taxi rank
outside Schiphol airport in March. 'Baker Street' by Gerry Rafferty
was playing and after forty years you were still in mourning, moaning
inwardly, letting every sound spill through and out of you like water.

New Year

I was in Jakarta for Lunar New
Year. It was colder than expected
but I still kept the air con on at
night and because of that and the
fact we weren't talking I sat up and
looked through messages on
my phone trying to work out if
there was some pattern there. It was
all about what to eat what to pick up
what to watch. The next day
at the museum Gedung Gajah
among the empty cases were two
clay figures the caption referred to
as a married couple from South
Sulawesi, a kind of toy played with
by girls. Look at that, I said, but
my grandma was in the cafe
in her wheelchair and you were in
Connecticut. Both figures had
little round nipples, one hugged
its knees, the other sat cross-legged,
their mouths small and angry. They
looked like children forced
to eat their soup. I thought of
the opening of *The Turin Horse*, the
narrator describing how Nietzsche
saw a horse being flogged and
flung his arms around the horse's
neck, sobbing and sobbing till a
neighbour took him home where
he lay in bed for two days before

uttering his final words: Mother, I am
stupid. I saw blank snow covering
the roads and on the branches
by your window, sad new faces
looking back at you on night walks
when the snow reflecting off
your torch was the colour of your
thoughts. Stupid so stupid. I couldn't
see to see. What are you looking at?

Voice Notes

Even if it could be named it would only be
as some token, some part-for-whole, of what
could be expressed. I was scanning the
walls for tokens, the high ceilings of
the Arndale Sports Direct, trying to reach
a white jumper. It rained non-stop, rain
through the window hitting my screen. I
wanted you to trust me. I drank a mug
of water. I slept to the sound of your voice
speaking in my phone thinking there must

be some token, some part-for-whole, that
could express this heart for yours, and the
next day I bought an orange bracelet from
Wong Wong Bakery on Princess Street.
I ate a honey bun. I wanted you to know
me, but it was easier to speak with no
intention of trying to know. Why do you
have this need to know? My room was damp.
I went to see Joe for a drink in town, in
my hands the actual token that comes from

the same root as *to teach*, which phases
in and out of being, existing inasmuch as
you want it. Parts of speech express our
parting. The wounded fall in the direction
of the wound. On the bus we passed
a little cenotaph on Ardwick Green, our
names incised on each stone face, and I don't
know why but I was thinking about when I
was five, staying with my mum in her dorm
at Peking University, huddled like prawns

under the duvet. I walked home with the
knowledge of your voice there waiting
for me. Speech you gave became my own.
Of all the data I thought of your name
next to mine. What does it mean to be
exposed, to speak? I thought of your
name next to mine, the token in our hands
that wouldn't speak without the thought
you'd hear it. You taught me language and
I love you for it. *What strategies do you have*

to keep calm and avoid triggers? Ben listened to
Ghostface Killah. I left the flat at half past
five. I ate tofu noodles in Stockport. I watched
The Day After Tomorrow. I woke to your
voice speaking in my phone, condensation
on the windows, damp patch growing by
the door. You called to blow a gust of falafel
my way, hummus and raw onions in the
trees. Sunlight after forty days of rain. Not
speaking, speaking. What does it mean

when suddenly, without warning, feelings
percolate? Coffee on the hob, a bag of bread.
There must be some token, some part-for-
whole, that could express this heart for
yours. When I got in I said I'm home and
you said yes I know and sat down next to me.
I thought of you learning crochet with
Samina, eating biscuits. I missed Tuesdays
painting with Cath. Politics wasn't just
in the language. It was in the garlic

chopped together, talking casually. I knew
the feeling. No one asked me how my
face and speech related. Morning answered
night. We existed in a phase of being
continuous with talking, with congee and
naptimes. I believed that when we spoke
a token would appear, a third space implied
by our voices, a plane of understanding
entered into, that we knew would stay.
I heard it. And I heard it in you speaking.

Coffee in October

I was at one of Allan Kaprow's first 'happenings' with
my brother who I hadn't seen in a long time, who I'd been
worried about. Someone led us up to a performance space
with high tattered ceilings. There weren't many of us, maybe
twenty or so. Office-style partitions had been put up,
dividing the room into separate cubicles. We were split
into groups of four by helpers wearing black leotards. My
brother asked to stay with me. We found a tray of water

and a ball of string, then heard a sound like tambourines.
A helper came in with a child's toy guitar but ducked out
again when he realised he had the wrong place. Another
told us to put one hand up against the partition wall
every time she said *now* and then said *now* several times
at random intervals. Afterwards, back on the street, my
brother asked if I'd understood it. I told him I don't
think it's about anything in the way you're asking. And

I could hear the helper saying *now*, her voice in my ear,
when I'd reached out and put my palm flat against the
flimsy partition wall, not knowing if you were in the next
cubicle over doing the same thing or if your hand would
be in the same place. But that connection I couldn't
see or hear stayed with me the next day as I was drinking
coffee, breathing through my blocked nose, associated
with the word *now*, linked in that moment of waiting, of

listening. It's fine, I told my brother. We all have those
thoughts. It's fine. Rain dotted the window of a chicken
shop. We hummed and held each other, October air
almost hyperreal in the way it sliced the streets in two.
And it happened, that feeling of being there, because
we couldn't see each other, or because I didn't know
you were there but chose to speak anyway, across the thin
partition that divides us, voices skittering into the open.

South London Mum

Halfway through our lease, a wealthy couple moved in next door. The husband wore a baseball cap and the wife blogged under the name South London Mum. Sometimes parcels got left at ours and the husband would come by, all smiling and hey guys. Those were our only real interactions except for this one time we were sitting out on the patio and for no reason Jenni threw a strawberry over her shoulder that flew straight into their garden and hit South London Mum. What the fuck! she shouted, and didn't really accept Jenni's apology. Last Saturday at Fred's Ale House someone told me how he'd woken up halfway down the street with Pablo next to him. He hadn't been drinking or anything. Ok maybe he'd had one. He was eating a lamb doner, ignoring the vibe. Someone else (a friend of a friend) told me about seeing a man in Chorlton with a wicker basket picking apples from his tree. That was when she said she knew she had to leave. I told her that we'd found the blog because of a parcel addressed to SOUTH LONDON MUM. It was around then they were redoing their kitchen and along with all the noise we had a mouse infestation. But nothing was acknowledged. They were always smiling on her feed. A mouse ate through a packet of crisps. Another we found cooked in the toaster. One night we couldn't sleep because of an argument between the husband and South London Mum. You ruined my life. You fucked it up. You fucked up my entire life. Stop crying you fucking baby. When I woke up I was halfway down the street with Pablo next to me. Ok so maybe I'd had a few but the weather was good. I told him that though Jenni hadn't meant to throw the strawberry at her she didn't care that she had. Pablo said his mum didn't pretend, English people pretend. It was sunny so we put our chairs outside and laughed at Mum.

Commute Songs

Days of palling taste preceding. Days
unchanging, changing just to take
the bins out. Then the cat stopped
eating and the hall light dimmed.
      I woke to wake-up in
      a cloudless dream, my
      tonsils rapt in cotton wool.
      The daybell rang. Loudly
      sang the cuckoo and
      downstairs a small leaf
      waited like a wooden boat.

                                          Once asking if she
                                          had something on
                                        her face she forgot
                                          the tubes clipped to
                                        her septum and turned
                                        with pride towards
                                          the surplus blossom
                                        on the trees outside.

Afterwards, what words. What
after. My watch stopped at the
beginning of the month. I gathered
sheaves instead and placed them at
the foot of an empty bed. For *U*,
I said, pretending vowels could best
be made to compensate for absent
friends. In sad rancour *O* chose not
to eat, drink or speak for thirty
days. So did *I* drink the flat earth dry
alone, until discovering a hair sealed
in a bag of flour, which must have
sprouted there. I called it *A*, no, *E*.
I asked if it would name itself for me.

Always I am talking to myself,
saying things like *commute* and
septum, as if I could out-think
the verray thought, while in a
corner of the screen, a corner
of myself retreating, hearing
stupid things me said, I wink.
        How can you grow
        without having shared
        your work, lodged
        in you like an unused
        parachute. An embolism.
Always the voice off-screen butts in.

When she died she fell to earth
so quickly neither the Gitane
nor wine glass fell from her hands.
        Vail'd and open were
        her eyes. The fire brigade
        broke in to find her
staring at the wall. But look at me.
But you weren't there. You're
laughing. Everyone is dead.

Gradations make it late,
no longer five to eight or
ten or midnight but actually –
in the sense of having always
been – late. So late I hear
a car honk from two days
ago, the driver calling bye,
I love you, bye in a hollow in
the wall above where once
a fluyt set sail, and I call
bye, I love you, bye. Between
the podcast and the lamp
memory dies. I hear the tent
flaps blow. An ambush laid
in sleep. Waves foam over
the beam ends. So many
gradations past the point
of not being late I hear you
calling and fall straight asleep.

I looked to the muck of
crumbs. The grease swirl
in the baking tray, rainbow-
girded, touching in its way.
The cat's uneaten food stuck
to her bowl. I almost ate it as
an example to her. Why
don't you eat? The fat robin
and the throbbing sky in gaps
between the branches. I left
it all and went to sit down
with my phone, both of us
     knowing what would
     happen. Ring it did.
     A strange noise
     warbling under me.

My grandam's work
unbegun stays with
me for a week and
hurries on. So do I
reparate the dead.
Tonight she's doing
the Banana Pancake
Trail. But I have hopes. One day
she'll lay her backpack down and
raise aloft the flag of unbecoming.
One day she'll taste authentic
satay. Till then in dreams she looks
on me and begs me please to wake.

I thought I saw a stock-dove.
I knewe not how to tearme it.
There were burpees. There were
people so absorbed in skipping
they could miss the woman rowing
silently. Queues formed around
   the corner. As the road is
   to the sea I would commute
   my life for you, so what is
   known might be as one
   withdrawing at the other's
   roar. Come daily to the rocks.
   Longed for or lost, love
   returns. Cross over to me.

       Such as it was
       a little span
       of knowing
       yet some do
       so astonne
       the limbs of
       them that
       toucht them.

The cat slumped on my dead leg.
I rubbed behind her ear. Checked
her breathing. Outside the new air
dusty. Many motes of dust. I fed
her first, made porridge soup,
drank coffee, ate a piece of toast
and came back up, by which time
all the dust had been sieved off.
        These songs began.

If I hold to any belief then what
    I hold to like a favourite leaf
is in there being some continuity
    of being. So where are you.

Weather and Address

If I can't reach you, let me fold these words into a better
concept of direction. I want to reclaim the horror of pure speech.
Walking down West Green Road to Seven Sisters, toggling
between street view and the view itself, snow makes everything
familiar, the sky falling upwards as you wheel your bike. Even the
familiar roads are treacherous. Last summer Hugh and I made an
autonomous zone on the pavement outside his flat with
an old sofa and a broken chest of drawers. He put his pot plants

on the wall, free to take, and that was it, a mode of address
emerging like the weather, not directed at but around us. Any
direction you took was walking away. The cost of walking away
was felt as a gag reflex, no spasm able to dislodge words once
spoken. So don't fucking say it. The harm perpetrated on speech
by the agents of media was clear. When we sat on that sofa
it was Parliament Square or Capitol Hill. Any place where enough
people have congregated and cried for no reason, the spirit

passing through them. The weather only appears to come from
above. When I write his name and delete it – when I write your
name and delete it – I understand the evil of speech for its
own sake. I don't address him. My eyes are dry as I imagine a
crow pecking at his corpse, the cops out in force smiling at
the dog owners. The important thing is that redemption can exist
alongside hate. We hear the wind change, stating its true direction.
I keep switching tabs, toggling views, not looking at you but

at the screen where our eyes meet, or later at the twitch in your face
mask as we talk. We've lived together long enough, in shared
isolation, in mutual address, speech more real for being mediated.
We know what mass is. A mode of talking through, of lightness
over meals. As weather makes contact with the ground, snow grains
spilling through our hands assuming resistance, we hear
ourselves as we exist, without any principle but that which reaches
beyond speech, because the sky surrounds us falling upwards.

I wanted the walls painted blue and the ceiling white to look
like Malcolm Campbell's *Blue Bird* which I used to look at
each night. On the top bunk next to me was a poster which
I got in a cereal box of every land speed record holder
since 1898, of which I liked the *Blue Bird* best. I liked
the top bunk because I'd get this feeling sometimes of
the night rising up around me. My brother would pass out
immediately. A speed sleeper. But when our parents fought
I looked at the *Blue Bird*. Recently, I discovered that
Malcolm Campbell kept a pennant from the British Union
of Fascists in his car. A blue background with a bolt of
white lightning. And now I wonder if that pennant meant
to him something like what the *Blue Bird* meant to me:
not a way to stop being scared but to move faster. A belief
that maybe if you break the speed of sound, sound itself
disappears. Brother, I can't hear you sleeping underneath me.

BROTHER POEM

Brother

there's a road I have to walk down
and I don't know what's at the end of it
and all we have between us

    1 bar of soap
    1 babybel
    1 yoyo

In the first memory I have
                    Dad rolls a cigarette
steerwheel between his knees when
        a cricket   wings beating
flings itself against
        the dashboard headrest windscreen

                and I strain against my harness
                        screaming *stop*
        baccy flying as he swerves
across two lanes

I can hear those legs *crrrrrrrrrrrrrrrrr*
        in my head
            I can't see to see
but my brother eyes wide
                holds his hands out
        patiently

                            Though we couldn't
                                know it we could feel it
                            that lull before
                                two stars collide
                                    Dad first then Mum
                            but hiding in the pipes
                                under the sink
                                    mighty
                                molecules we were
                            our every action as
                                beautiful or
                                indistinct
                                    as the globules
                                        in a lava lamp

give it back to me give it back
give me it give it to me give it
back give it back to me give it

gaaaaaaaaaaaaaaaaaaaa
aaaaaaaaaaaaaaaaaaa
aaaaaaaaaaaaaaaaa
gaaaaaaaaaaa
gaaaaaaaaaaa
gaaaaaaaaaaaaaa
gaaaaaaaaaaaaaa
gaaaaaaaaa
gaaaaaaaaaaa
gaaaaaaaaaaa
ga
ga
ga

take it take it
take it take it take
it take it take it

Brother
it's a funny
word to say or
to address to you as if
you were here because if you were
I wouldn't be saying it that's what's funny

Brother
more a question
than a name with the
implication being do you have a brother
what does your brother do where is your brother

Brother
a frozen word
like being on the other
side of a locked door one of
those walk-in freezers where they
hang big slabs of meat *brrrrr* I'm outside
standing by the airtight door whispering through
each steel hinge what was that you'll have to speak up
I can't hear a word you're saying no I can't hear anything

BROTHER
    BROTHER
        BROTH–
before I knew your
    face or name
I saw the moons
    of spring
    fatal   moons
which for days
    on end became
whatever was most
    unkind till
    in a voice so
    in a shapeless
flame an image
    in excelsis came
and clear enough
    to make the old
    world groan
there you were
    open and sublime
    a bundle
of saliva waiting
    to be kissed

Brother did we really
communicate as
particles we shrank
down to the size of

going unseen as we
raced between
the stacked plates
vibrating fast enough

to make the dust
just dance dance
just above the blue
surface of the sofa

On the wrong side of the glass
    the doors slid shut
and off we went
                you never cried
        but that day
your round face white with fear
    mirrored mine
I ran back to find you
        sitting on the shoulders
of a tall white man

and you cried at the sight of me as if
you knew I meant to carry you away
which of course I did

On the first night I stood
   in front of the bathroom
mirror chanting

       BROTHER
          BROTHER
            BROTH–

but a trapped animal noise
   echoed off the tiles
and took me by the arm
   and I jumped back into bed

On the second night
   I stood there again each bead
of sweat on my neck moonlit
   wet hair combed back

   BROTHER
     BROTHER
      BROTH–

And when I exhaled
   a glass pitcher smashed
in the kitchen but Mum
   wouldn't believe me

On the third night

    BROTHER
        BROTHER
           BROTHER

I spoke plainly and waited
   in a silence so deep I knew
you must be listening
   but you wouldn't speak

so I leaned over the sink and
   drank straight from the tap

        Look look
        I said
            I can't

        This is what
        it looks like

        I take
            you take

        but not from
        the same place

My collection of stones
kept carefully wrapped
in a Clarks shoebox
under the stairs a dozen
different coloured gems
pink green lilac all
mine not yours but I
let you hold them even
my favourite rose quartz
which you said you'd
seen before me though
only after you lost it

You came to me as three
white lakes each whiter
than the other this is how
my mind goes when
        I look at the sky
    I call the captain
tall my face and lie down
by the water brother
        you know I know
    nothing

One day we saw a man singing
outside his front door

            No said Mum
he doesn't live there that's where
his mum lived when she was alive
that's why he's singing there

          Every poem is another
          poem that didn't make it

          that in trying to write
             the liquid crystal of my
             eye shut out

          behind whose silence
          crackles the poem
             I could be writing

          which in writing takes
             the place of you

Mum near Covent Garden
　　dragging her feet after work
　　　buys a top she'll never wear
　　and trudges home to find us
sitting in front of the tv
　　cottage pie back in the oven
　　　whatever it was
　　that crossed her mind
　　　　　transposed
　　rage solo
　　　at a different pitch
low enough to be
　　inaudible　 we turn
the volume up
　　　still light at half 8
　　the curtains drawn

　　　　　　The first poem I wrote was in my
　　　　　mind
　　　　　　　looking outside while
　　　　　　　　　　my parents
　　　　　fought　 my brother hiding
　　　　　　　　　under the bed

　　　　　　a paleblue thought in our
　　　　　mother's mind moving too fast
　　　　　　　to be caught

Between the devil and
the deep of Dad's snore
Mum's teeth gnashing

Between the deep blue
domes of two dead jellyfish
the soundwave of your breath

Low low pillow clutched
tightly to my ears every
evening sleeptime comes
and all the bands go drum

Grow grow let me grow
like mighty Robogoat
and if I get a wink tonight let
my dreams be numb

Woe woe willow boat
carry me away high
above the angry sky where
life is but a crumb

I liked the mist
but we agreed it
was a bad day
for a beach trip
all the windows
rolled down low
small droplets
of icc in her eyes

Our snapped-off shadows
made a simple shape
one within the other like
a folded napkin and you
talked to me in your real

voice I wanted to make
the dust just no I couldn't
couldn't see us all there
eating instant noodles
sitting in front of the tv

From Beaver Creek
to Uplift we shot
anything that moved
the birds singing
in the artificial
trees the true self
nothing more than
the self as seen

Brother you wanted the red
spade but you were
too small to swim and Mum
wouldn't let me go in without it

That autumn I picked a red
felt-tip pen and made a circle
with a curling line attached

A neighbour had been giving
or receiving singing lessons
and they sounded like a couple
arguing
              Do re mi!
                          shouted one
the other spat in his eye

A panda walks into a bar
eats a sandwich then kills
a man and I'm sitting
two stools down when the
bartender asks why did you
do that and the panda
leans over and kills him
too

Then the next day the panda
walks into the bar again I
happen to be in the cloakroom
looking for your scarf trying
to understand these recurring
dreams in which you return
to me dressed as a panda
sit down and pull out a gun
but now I'm waiting outside
our house aged six thunder
in the pavement tree

Brother the night was
full and on my lips no
stars but names where
the dead leaf fell there
did it rest and the tree
being one leaf less
words filled the gap

Brother I talked to all
the dead whose names
were mine I talked
till there was no one
left I talked in you
and you in me till sleep
talked through us
both   be with me   be

Another bad year
moving backwards
turning as poets
turn from what it
was had moved us

Brother next to me
shutters open for
landing pointing out
the pandan trees
and Ciliwung as we
descend through
smog and rain again

I heard the door close
light left the room
            behind us

We were stuck
    in the museum

The others had names
they were the owners
    of their faces

But we met as strangers
    words in place of
            speech

Whichever way
    they held us to
the light we looked
    the same

I want to speak but also
to wander at peace myself

outdoors a green tree reading
in the free air having had

the elements in me language
porous with battered

lapsed impossible things
and after some time like this

though I don't have much
I want to come back

You said cemeteries were like
    funfairs without the candyfloss

Some days I'd go there to watch
    the milk plume in my tea

When the sun shone my tummy
    rumbled

        I was searching for
your name among the tombs

On the wrong side of the glass
    the doors slid shut
and off you went
           I never cried
    but that day
my round face white with fear
    mirrored yours
you ran back to find me
        sitting on the shoulders
of a tall white man

and I cried at the sight

I made the mistake of needing to pee
   and then deciding to shave and looking

myself right in the mirror features
   realigned to form a pattern that was

I-not-I the tap stopped running
   though my hand could feel the water

scalding I was holding a small car
   but what seemed wrong was that my

brother reached across the I-not-I
   we were planning a new heist you

were first to go I was lookout
   water started rising from all sides

so we wedged a table up against
   the door and waited wading knee-deep

through our room don't worry
   don't worry a small car in your hand

Impossible to picture it without crying the market with the petting goat

place you & the little goat in the market your little hand petting it again

in its little pen the photo of us at the market petting the little goat the

market that must exist for photos of little goats & the pen with which I

On the sofa in front of the tv
   I could be there
right now but for this
bottle of wine between us
and the fact I'm eighteen

What kind of party is this?
   Trying to unscrew
a bottle cap
   I know where I am
I don't know why
   I keep wishing I could be
     a speck of dust
in someone's eye
     pure memory

   I don't want to
move or speak just
   to impede the flow
   of light through
your cornea
     slightly

Brother you
tower over
me as over all
my worldly
goods and out
spills a piece
of paper
decorated
with a flower
printed with
your name

You say I
love her I'm *in*
love I LOVE
her all in one
outward breath
as you throw
your bag down
books and folders
spilling onto
the carpet which
is warm milk
beneath you

You saw me play *Final Fantasy VII*
    crush my head between my pillows
    listen to talk radio
    watch *Futurama*
    and

the shadow of your foot waved
    at me from the wall
you saw me falling backwards

    With foreign voices other
      willows conversed

    I was quiet
      as if I'd lost
    a brother

Brother is a section of the waiting art

is a section of the brother art waiting

a waiting brother art is section of the

section art is the waiting brother of a

brother of the art is a waiting section

the section brother is of waiting art a

waiting the section art of a brother is

art is a section of the waiting brother

One morning my door
  handle stared back at me
  vacantly its horizontal
gaze like glass unable
obviously to tell
  if I was sitting in bed
  making eye contact
with you since from
its flat perspective
  everything was past we
  might as well be playing
with our blue diplodocus
taking too long in
  the bath sharing equal
  blame for our parents'
sad happy fates knowing
no future existed and
  neither did we

  And as
  I walked on
  though my life was
  broken yes my voice was
  heard and it my voice I heard
  in a little corner of the room saying
  I'll walk with you and leave you with me

BUS
     BUS
         BUS

I said it like that and like that
a bus appeared
so leaning on the glass
I started saying

    BROTHER
       BROTHER
       BROTHER

            That game again but this time
               nothing

            And the next day in
            Aldi staring at the floor
              thinking about
            what vegetables to buy
            you came up behind me

              It's been a while

            I dropped my basket
            and you handed me a cabbage
            which I ate as a dog would
              without asking why

You thought a picnic might be
coming on too strong but by then
I'd already bought the bread and
hummus and borrowed someone's
bike and stopping near a field
of crows she took a photo then we
cycled on till I got a puncture so
we walked the whole way home and
did shots sitting cross-legged
on her carpet and when it
came to leaving I wheeled
my bike down to the sea
past empty shops and cafes
vodka humming inside me
I could see where things began
you were happy

What will I do
in the future

Use I or him
when I mean you

Brother it was last week but
I'm five
        we read the sky for
signals rose quartz means rain
at night but never avoiding
    rough seas we yes *we*
lead ourselves to the jetty
hand in hand empty as a weeto
boats like rabid ski dogs
    shhhhhhh   we can't be out
this late
            but you yes you
are setting sail by this point
                only you

                    He looked down with such
                        sadness he couldn't bring
                    himself to call out to a
                    member of the crew it was
                    too overwhelming to be
                        helped and too simple

                    to bear it was the thought
                    that finally struck him as
                    he looked up at the captain
                        and with great sadness
                    looked back at his brother
                    still unable to see it

Fin of light
I know you care
over and above
  the stairwell
  the outdoor
    gym

  there you go
    not cloud or
    shadow
        just

If you
freeze water it
becomes solid if you
speak something it
conveys
something

even in
this moon crater
whose rough
winds I dedicate
to you

Address and Weather

the face of England

You suggested a drink, so I met you at the shop. Your shift had just ended. Realising that it was 'Brexit Day' we decided to walk in the direction of Parliament. Things were dying down, crowds heading back towards Westminster Station. Then a fight broke out in front of McDonald's. Police officers on horseback dragged a screaming man away. We reached Parliament Square. Two women were in tears. They stood next to Churchill, tote bags swinging by their sides, and sang the service of my love the love that asks no questions. I told you I was tired. I couldn't get anything down in writing. I recorded myself speaking into my phone as I fell asleep. The only important word was *flagon*

It's me! It's me!

You were talking about losing control of speech. I was in my last year of university. We had heard that on All Souls' Day people prayed for the dead and for souls trapped in purgatory. Near midnight, we sat and wrote poems. The previous summer I'd made friends with someone in the Midwest. Her mum was also an immigrant. We drank coffee in church as she talked about her brother who died in a road accident. That was when she found God. His wife had become pregnant soon after. She had a little niece. It was a miracle. And now she spoke through me, the moon visible behind the clouds

the cops waiting

You told me about your dream of falling. I didn't understand what it meant. Anxiety? Bad posture? An unspeakable need? I'd been recording myself falling asleep. At the same time, I was watching a lot of bad films. It occurred to me that the dialogue in these films resembled someone talking under hypnosis. In *Next*, Nicolas Cage and Jessica

Biel are driving from Las Vegas to Flagstaff talking about the weather (it's raining) and then about Denmark and fish eggs. The dream becomes part of the day's residue

a plate of green smog

You were sceptical about things easing. In the park we agreed that summer rain was 90% memories, 10% water. And who could speak from a subject position with such vague contours, which implied such a uniformity of experience? I wanted to reject belonging. In doing so, to find new forms of solidarity. But this came out of feeling rejected. My granddad helped protect others during the massacre. You told me that. After being released from prison, he took the family to Jakarta. That too. The government banned the use of Chinese names. Mum's name was changed. Yes I know. Yes. This is separate from me but the feeling isn't

gunk

You were with me through the turbulence, the red seat belt light turned on. It's ok, I said, and my addressing this to you made it ok. On either side of me were strangers. The next day, I was in the crematorium in Tangerang staring at a photograph of my granddad in a tiny glass cubicle. The smell of cloves mixed with the tinny saxophone sound on the speakers. I filmed my grandma looking at him. I was looking at him with you

the colour of your thoughts

You thought my need represented a lack and there was a difference between a gap and a boundary and I left my grandma to walk through the museum. The access lever in me was broken. You quoted words to the effect that words were made to prevent us near. A noun is an imperfect substitute for a pronoun. But it wasn't distance. I felt it as an ache in my lower abdomen *in the direction of the wound*

You take what hurt you and hold it against the hurt parts of your body. Sometimes, by a kind of sympathetic magic, healing feels possible. But I don't know what I'm doing, or know just enough – scraps of poems, conversations, family stories – to make it work briefly, though I always speak so badly. I hate talking out loud

through my blocked nose

You remind me of what Lotte said in connection to Allan Kaprow, words to the effect that movement happens in moments of collectivity, if not a totalising unison of. Art was like the weather

halfway down the street with Pablo

You suggested a drink, so you met me at the library. Realising that it was 'Brexit Day' we decided to walk in the direction of Parliament. Things were heating up, crowds flowing out of Westminster Station. Then a fight broke out in front of McDonald's. Police officers on horseback galloped past. We reached Parliament Square. Two women were laughing. They stood next to Churchill, tote bags swinging by their sides, and sang the service of my love the love that asks no questions. You told me you were tired. You couldn't get anything down in writing. You recorded yourself speaking into your phone as you fell asleep. The only important word was *baby*

The grease swirl in the baking tray

You didn't know my friend who died. Early in the year. I hadn't known her long. Grief was embarrassing. An anthropologist refers to a zig-zag model of time, whereby time is not so much a straight line as a sequence of oscillations between polar opposites: night day winter summer drought flood age youth life death. In such a scheme, the past has no *depth* to it. All past is equally past. It is simply the opposite of future. Before her death, time was abstract. A blanket concealing the crumbs of day-to-day. Now I felt time in my body. Time stretched out when my teeth ached or when I thought of family. Stopped briefly in the morning. Slowed down again at night. Solidly, fluidly

the cost of walking away

You asked about my encounter with the man. The man with the post-gym look. With new trainers and an expensive white tee. Minimal eye contact. Questions questions. Evil stubble. He wanted help understanding things. He wanted to know what I thought. Help me unpack this. At what point does an opinion become a fact? The moment it leaves you. To stand at this border exhausts our power of listening and makes us aware of a crisis. You are more or less real than the entrance to Blackwall Tunnel. You're still talking

a pennant

You found an image which fell out as you opened this book, quoting a line to the effect that photography was not a question (a theme) but a wound. I fell asleep surrounded by soft toys. You were asking when this was. When nothing else worked. When the threat was falling Outside

above the angry sky

You were invented for the purpose of You were crying because You wanted to exist but You were scared You stole things You ran away You didn't come back You cried and no one came You shrank until only I could see you You wanted to be but You couldn't describe it You were scared You had to be dragged outside You noticed stillness You wanted to write You consulted a book You broke down internally You wrote the same word again and again You left because You left because You couldn't speak except You could You had no idea You were the point You couldn't be

Take the origin of banal: a
bannal-mill where tenants
carried their corn to be ground
for the benefit of the lord. But
imagine it without the lord, all
of us taking our corn to the mill
saying I'm sad, I'm lonely,
I can't take it, and then grinding
the corn, baking it, sharing it.
I eat if you eat. Maybe it's the
knowledge of what's shared –
or could be – that stops me on
the point of exposure, of breaking
down, because I can't let go of
feelings, of the belief in a singular
self without which I disappear,
or hear you speaking with my
mouth, my pain in yours. Why
do you write? I saw you standing
on the corner with a bag of food.
When the lights changed it was
summer and we were by the river,
talking. I was trying to explain why
writing is pointless, but you were there.

The point of writing is to address
you. It's so embarrassing to
talk like this. At the checkout
I forgot what I had to buy.
Another memory appeared like
washing-up liquid replaced by
fizzy drinks, a feeling that didn't
begin with me. And I pictured
you saying this to yourself as
you waited on the corner with
a bag of food, also having
forgotten some obvious thing, its
place taken by the image of
a river green with scum, fish
floating to the surface in a sudden
trance. You couldn't work out
where it was or who was talking
but the fact it happened made us
both feel calm. So we decided,
standing there, to regard all
our feelings as mutual, the only
action as collective, and speech
a way of taking it to you.

Acknowledgements

This book is an experiment in talking sideways. As such, there are many sibling figures and texts that sit behind and alongside it.

Some of *Brother Poem* appeared elsewhere in different forms: 'In June, outrageous stood the flagons . . .' was in *The Beef Onion* (The Minutes, 2020); 'In Anxiety Dreams' in *Project Self-Detective* (ed. Grace Linden); 'After "The Quinine Plant"' in *East Side Voices* (ed. Helena Lee); 'Free Will' in *The New Republic*; 'New Year' in *Granta*; 'Commute Songs' in the exhibition *An Incomplete A to Z for Art and Poetry* (curated by Rachael Allen and Guy Robertson); 'Weather and Address' as the film 'Like Cockroaches' on Episode 1, Season 3 of Transmissions TV (curated by Hana Noorali, Anne Duffau and Tai Shani); parts of 'Brother Poem' in *SPAM*, a commission from The Poetry Society, *All This Is Implied* (HappenStance, 2017), *RENDANG* (Granta, 2020), *The Scores*, People of Letters (curated by Melanie Abrahams); and the final poem ('Take the origin of banal . . .') in *Tentacular*. Thank you to all the editors and curators.

Many of the poems also appeared in four pamphlets made during a residency hosted by Mahler & LeWitt Studios in Spoleto (thank you to Guy, Typhaine, Tomasso, Rachael, Sophie, Felix, Marie, Ceci, Lynton, Hana).

Thank you to Jennifer Reeser for permission to quote from her translation of Anna Akhmatova's 'Willow' in the epigraph. 'Coffee in October' draws from a dream-inflected memory of a scene from Samuel Delany's *The Motion of Light in Water*. Some other texts drawn from include: Susan Stewart, *Poetry and the Fate of the Senses*; Elias Canetti, *The Secret Heart of the Clock*; Sigmund Freud, *The Interpretation of Dreams*; John Ashbery, 'The Double Dream of Spring'; Ben Jonson, *The Devil is an Ass*; Levinus Levnius, *The Touchstone of Complexions* (trans. Thomas Newton); George Chapman, *The Iliads of Homer*; J.H. Prynne, 'In Cimmerian Darkness'; Amiri Baraka, 'Betancourt'; Veronica Forrest-Thomson, 'Sonnet'; Charles Sanders Peirce, *The*

Collected Papers, Vol. II: Elements of Logic; Anne Carson, *Economy of the Unlost*; Edmund Leach, *Culture and Communication*; Roland Barthes, *Camera Lucida*; John Lyly, *Sapho and Phao*; Allan Kaprow, *7 Environments*; Lotte L.S., 'The We of A Position'.

Thank you to all the friends and poets who are part of this book. Thank you for letting me quote you, Ben. Thank you John, Bryony, Lydia, Nell, and James in Manchester. Thank you to everyone at the Extra Care homes in Tower Hamlets (Cath and Lisa especially). Thank you to the social poetics group (Lotte and Mau!); to Anna, Hannah and Richard (faces!); to Belinda, Gboyega, Keith, Victoria, Ray and Rosemary; to Jay, Nisha and Mary Jean; to Joe and Hugh. Thank you to Aisha, my sibling heart. Thank you Niki and Rachael, as always. Thank you to Suzanna, Jackie and Stephanie at Wesleyan, and to Christine and Isabella at Granta.

This book is dedicated to my parents Yenny and Arthur, and to all imaginary siblings.

© Matthew Thompson

WILL HARRIS is a London-based poet of Chinese Indonesian and British heritage. His first poetry book, *RENDANG*, was a Poetry Book Society Choice, shortlisted for the T. S. Eliot Prize, and won the Forward Prize for Best First Collection. He co-runs the Southbank New Poets Collective with Vanessa Kisuule, and works in care homes in Tower Hamlets.